Freedom of Expression

Freedom of Expression

Chase Freeheart

VANTAGE PRESS
New York

FIRST EDITION

Published by Vantage Press, Inc.
516 West 34th Street, New York, New York 10001

Manufactured in the United States of America
ISBN: 0-533-14069-2

Library of Congress Catalog Card No.: 01-126929

0 9 8 7 6 5 4 3 2 1

To God,
for without the gift that he
has given me, this book
would not be possible.

Contents

About the Author

Chase Freeheart is the author of several prize-winning poems, including "Mirror Reflections." Chase draws most of his poetry from his own life experiences and from those whom he has encountered while in the course of his career.

The effect of his poetry will make you re-think your own life as you journey along with him, experiencing a broad range of emotions from laughter to tears, rejoicing, and salvation. Chase embraces the soul as well as the mind with his acute observations on everyday life.

Chase Freeheart was born in a small town in Oklahoma. He traveled to many states as well as abroad until he began his military career in the United States Air Force at the age of twenty-one. At the conclusion of his career, he settled in Riverside, California, where he married, raised children, and divorced. His occupation took him to the Las Vegas, Nevada, area, where he currently resides, to write his thought-provoking poetry.

Freedom of Expression

Beach

The horizon reached up to meet the sun
The sun stood on tiptoes to see me saying good-bye
Then nestling into the horizon's breast for the night
Tripped over a piece of driftwood
Feeling its shape with my hands
The involuntary sculpture formed by an unseen hand
Quality enough to sit on my mantel
I could see the sky bunnies bounding
With their fluffy tails in bright light contracts
I feel the crunch of the wet sand beneath my feet
Forming a pattern of footsteps
Criss-crossing avoiding the incoming waves
I place this memory to be brought forward as needed.

Castigating

Loose your tongue and let your bitterness flow
Dragging those around with you to your level
Castigating those who don't meet your needs
All consuming to your way of life.
Your life is a dead organism trying to give life.

Change Is the Same

Raindrops collide with each other
Form a trickle at the end of the leaf.
The smell of fresh mown hay merges with the smell of the
    mist
Walking alone the country road.
Frolicking colts kick up their heels
Summertime is a good time to be alive.
Searching the different possibilities of the coming fall.
Extended summer merges into the fall spectrum of colors.
Artists delight in the activity of the falling leaves.
Alive and well are the key
Words of life.
Ever changing and always the same.

Cleansing

The rain in my mind is cleansing
Overflowing the closures of containment
Releasing the dross that has held my thinking stagnant
Leaving the watercolor pastels of pureness
Learning how to process pain
The silent pain is gone
Arousing contentment in compassion for others
Feeling their pain, just to listen.

Clusters of Nonsense

Clusters of nonsense raise the hair on my neck
Storing the information in places forgotten
Rallied and viewed sometimes from afar
Blown out of proportion in limited time schedules
But those little things can bring a smile to my face
Maybe a tear to my eye in comfort.

Colors

The sounds of light awaken my day
Placing colorful patterns of light in places of energies
The color of water modifies my facial content
Its color of coolness splashed across my face
The color of my dog in uncontrolled love
The color of grass between my toes
The color of milk and cookies
Red pasta sauce rolling across my tongue
Money green converts into the smell of enjoyment
Flesh tones convert into the feel of softness.

Confused

My hands are tied
Depression at my side
Dragging my life through a ringer
I have no control that's the stinger.

When did I lose control?
It's taken its toll
Oh, just to live one more day with a smile
Oh, to lift my steps to go one more mile.

It hit me in the face to make me confused
How can you stand there and look so amused?
I need to take control and not let my mind pay
Time heals all wounds holding depression at bay.

Crying on the Inside

I'm crying on the inside
    But what a smile I can give you on the outside.
Hopin' that you won't notice what I'm hiding
    Divided in my thinking and my writing.

Viewing from the top of the mountain
    Walking on my tiptoes drawing from my youth
    fountain.
I draw an imaginary heart to my breast
    I give an imaginary kiss, I guess I'm not at my best.

Somehow I catch your eye as I walk by
    I watch you out of the corner of my eye.
I see you suppress your urge to say hello
    I'm really excited but I seem to so mellow.

I picked up something you had dropped
    My greeting was shallow and flopped
Fumbling with clever words is not my nature
    You seem so much, much more mature.

Dancing

Don't dance on my twinkle toes
    When we dance around the floor, I should know,
That as light you are on your feet
    It would be a treat.

To twirl around the floor
    And not exit through the door.
Being lost in your charm
    One dance could do no harm.

The Cha Cha Cha, the Mambo, and the Fox Trot,
    My feet touched the floor more often than not.
The merengue, the limbo, and the two-step, too.
    My, how the evening flew.

To see your smiling face,
    You limped just a trace.
You whispered to me while afoot,
    "You need just one right foot."

Day Start

Coffee cup held between two hands
Lifting it to smell the difference it makes in my life
The vapor surrounds my smell cells
Going in, around, and through
Holding it, holding it
Dragging through the nostrils until full lung capacity
Eyes closed and smiling
Allowing the brown life liquid to fill my mouth
Flowing back and forth, back and forth
Doing its destined duty
My life force pump driving the caffeine to its destined
    purpose
Rejuvenating those sleepy cells
My daydream has started.

Diet

Dieter's dream
Lettuce main course
Frozen scale
Attitude
Compulsory reaction
Eating binge
Dieter's reward.

Divorce

Met you at the place to file divorce today
Hopes for a better future are being placed there
One little slip put us here
What is being gained but an empty life without another?
Never to have the pleasure that we had
Never to walk through time
Placing our feet in the hourglass residue
A silent reminder of ourselves.

Don't Cry

Don't cry for me.
    Hidden inside this meek exterior is a man like a tree.
The tears that I shed are a release from the joy hidden
    inside.
    I laugh at comforting tones and someone who stands
    beside.

The shadow cast from the inward tree,
    Overshadows those around me.
Don't touch me or you may feel the cold,
    Of the hours of happiness untold.

Don't Say Good-bye, But I'll See You

We test the soil as we stand at the graveside's edge
    That we may not fall in and lose our life too soon.
The fullness of life is still not a dredge
    In the quagmire of our job we don't cry out in our
    gloom.

We say good-bye to a friend and we'll see you soon.
    Turning our thoughts to more pleasant things,
We stuff our faces at the wake and enjoy the boon.
    With alcohol and drugs we free ourselves with altered
    wings.

Our newly found freedom we follow our dream.
    Doing exotic trips, fine clothes and tapping our
    essence.
Now in our fullness of finery we're a part of the team.
    One more item to buy and our credit card is maxed.
    This doesn't make sense.

Depression sets in and makes our dreams shallow.
    We see the shadow of ourselves that we want to be.
This lump in our throat makes it hard to swallow.
    One trip to the Bankruptcy Court and the cycle begins
    again. Don't you see?

Emerging

Dreams to be fulfilled
Lost in the moment of time
Graduated time schedule
Focusing on the impurities of lost time
Many levels of unnoticed implications
Guarded meaningful compliments
Lifeline extended covers lost moments of time
Blank stares trying to find strength from solace
Seasons of gloom drift by into temporal happiness
Breaking into the days of sunshine and a new outlook
Modified thinking lifts spirits to another level
Merging of simple times and uncomplicated lifestyles
Closing eyes and viewing the emerging future.

Emptiness

I felt the emptiness knocking at my door
I felt her walking away to a cold nothingness
Longing for that closeness
Those conversations we had
I shudder in the darkness
Loneliness is overwhelming
Awakened to reality by the demand for attention by my
    cat.

Eyes Romanced

Romancing those eyes
Romancing those blue eyes
The eyes that view me in a different light
Building my confidence in life
The hue of love, as a rose,
Stands alone, a symbol of love
A fragrance that dreams are made of.

Exposure

Who/what am I?
Crying tears of exposure
Trying to hide from self
Going to places never gone before
Crying tears of exposure
Incidentals hidden in my suitcase of life
Fortuitous happenings I changed daily
Don't hold me back in my search for life.

Freedom

Freedom to walk my path alone
To seek pleasures in other ways
Carrying my load on weakened shoulders
Rubbing those battle scars
Being thankful that I pulled through okay
Holding my head as high as possible
Trying not to look over my shoulder
Focusing on what lies in the future
Pushing doubts away into a new life.

Freedom Is

Compulsory reaction to fear
    such brings me a tear.
Hold still feet, but my knees are knocking
    and my teeth are a-clicking.
Hold on, now it's time to straighten my back
    and do the things I cannot hack.
Show the plan. Show the plan. Show the plan.
    After all I did take a stand
To build that dream that no one can see but me.
    I'll hold onto life, build a dream, and get free.

Free Spirit

Free to be about, around, and through things
Life expectancy unknown
To move through time riding an asteroid
With no air, wind blowing through my hair
Being drawn into a black hole
Seeing ancient worlds consumed
Remnant spacecraft compressed there in time
Released by my "free spirit" to surf on the Sun
Enjoyed wipe outs with my friends
Thoughts bring me back to reality in my garden.

Friends

You look at me in that special way
I turn my head with a grin
Schoolboy flutter in my heart
Run/stay run/stay
Is there another option?
Greased lighting hits my feet
Dust has settled before you turn around
Before I can tell those lies
The ones you want to hear
I feel no remorse
After all we're friends.

Friendship

The rushing of time going by only seems like yesterday
The joys and sorrows have been shared by all
The limitations of foresight would say
Friendships will end as you go your way
The friendship bonds flirt with destiny hidden in your
    mind
Until happiness brings them forth again
Thanks for being my friend.

Grace Me

Grace me with your feminine beauty
With your eyes see the pureness of my heart
I lay it before you
Unbounded, unlimited love
To be held to your breast
All I ask is yours in return.

Grandmother

The rustle of the trees about us
We sit at our table of contentment
A glance deep into her eyes
Things unknown were said in them
Conversations all around us unheard
Pictures of grandchildren
We shared your love for them
A tear forms to your tenderness
The gentleness while you view the newness of life
Subtle changes that only a grandmother can see
The mildness of her soft touch returns them to their folder
A life, a love, separate from the life she lives.

Grandeur

Grandeur of the past
Modified to meet today's needs
Altered personality
Struck with awe
Faster than we can think
Y2K problem solved
I listen to stories on my radio.

Guaranteed Difference

When I show my face
My face is a façade
Sculptured by time
Flowing free
Wearing my watch upside down
Rebelling the notions of lost time
Molding thoughts and actions to wants of others
Time changes not by the sunset
But by pleasing of others
My heart skips a beat when a smile appears
Time is not reversed by turning the hour glass
Not the sound of a clock
But free-flowing sand
Gives a false sense of security
Because no sound is made
And the time is lost forever.

Hands

With these hands I touch the softness of your skin
To see something I need to touch it
The eyes of my fingers see those unspoken words of your
    heart.
They caress those fears away
They give you confidence in those times of uncertainties
They give you strength when you are tired
A squeeze of your hand, you give me a knowing smile
I rub my fingers across your soft lips and feel the passion
    there.
With a touch I feel your awareness of me
I feel those unspoken passings between two people.

Heart Sounds

Love is the music of the heart
Painting pictures on our lifescape's adventures
On the seasons of lifetimes
Love floating on the gentleness of a soft kiss
Amazed at what life passions a passionate kiss is
In-depth eye contact
Searching for meanings
A walk in the full moon at midnight
A newness of youth
Amused at little things that were unnoticed before
I know nothing of these feelings
They control me, not me them.

Hiding the Truth

Hollowlike eyes make people seem invisible
I feel their presence and feel their stares
Turning my back I feel their aura of mistrust
Eyes pounding on my back
Creates fear and self-imposed illness
This lessens my fortitude of aggression
Makes me feel like a grain of discolored sand in a massive
    universe
The unpenetrating, invisible wall is cold and uninviting
Somehow I'm drawn to it doing fish face against its
    exterior.

I Chose Life

A suppression of my cells
    Delinquent until the end
Reaching the end of my rope
    I let go and fell flat on my face
I picked myself up and looked around
    At the many friends I had found
I brought them to my breast
    And lingered them with words unbound.
Tested and marred I held my head high,
    For I survived the crunch.
I believe as I move on that I'm a much happier man,
    For I stuck with the plan.
I chose life.

I See Red

What happens when they say there's no help?
When they just lie there in their pool of blood
They, in their weakened condition, reach out a hand
Help passes by for one more fortunate
A mother's child lies in its coldness
The flies aren't choosy
Bouncing from one corpse to another
Icy cold stares get no response from the body bag
A life has ended not to be shared again
Only in memory.

Idle Talk

Caught in eyes of those who say
"What harm will it do with a little slant on the truth?"
To hide behind their window shades
With idle talk during Bingo
To talk without looking
Not drawing attention to themselves
Dispersed to spread like wildfire
What harm would it do
Sobbing on my pillow
My friend comforts me
Things seem better now until tomorrow.

Introduction

Introduction to love
Hyperventilating
In case of fire, Break Glass
Emergency Exit Only.

Kiss

Extracting the essence of pleasure from your kiss
Holding my breath, toes curled
Eyes tightly closed
Receiving all that's possible in feelings
Clouds drift to their unknown destinies
My path is lit with the brightness of the sun
Pleasure smiles
My mindsight sees the future.

Life's Pages

Blind eye's vision
Not seeing the uncovering of the present
Each page written moment by moment
Can create joy or sorrow
New experiences, two never the same
Pages not numbered by memory
But brought forth as needed
Mind's eye spectrum of colors translates into experiences.

Life's Still the Same

Isolated area with a pond
Viewing the image I stand toe-to-toe with
The reflection is a perfect impression of me
The wooded area is solitude for thoughts
Have I changed that much from what seems yesterday?
My hair blends into the whiteness of the clouds
Touching the surface of the natural mirror
I am distorted, but still the same
Life's experiences may give areas of escape,
But I'm still the same person when things return to norm.

Love Is What?

What is this thing in my heart?
It wakes me in the middle of the night.
Cries out to no avail.
Displaying fits of anger,
At times displaying intelligence of a sort.
Who said love?
Who can say love and be serious?
Maybe that's what it is,
Cold sweats,
Heat flashes,
Numbness,
Yes, that's what it is.
Why would it grow anymore than it has?
Such a small heart to be holding such a large thing.
Do I have two hearts?
One that generates my brain,
The other hidden in my life force pump.

Love Passed By

Love is the merging of the likes and dislikes to make one
Fond touching, with closed eyes
Knowing what the other person is thinking
Doing for the other before it's asked
Small surprises in your favorite color
Knowing that facial expression and prepared to comfort
Miscounting cookies in your favor
Who changes when love changes?
Do we go back to separating our likes and dislikes?
When the facial expression is still the same,
Do we say, "Oh, no, not again?"
Where does love go, is there a love boneyard?
What are the feelings that are piled on top of those bones?
When we try to bring love back, what are the pitfalls?
Can we get to the same level of love again?
Can our love go even deeper?

Love Past By

That interglow disappears floating on a cloud of
    discontent
Faltering relationships seek other's help
Using them as a crutch
Using them as a shelter from the storm
Temporarily there's relief
The hurricane hits and no time to look for the eye
That limited time relationship becomes soul mates
Any problems they have are invisible
Focusing only on the departed spouse
The wound gets deeper
Children have to make decisions, which do we love?
Someone is the winner, someone is the loser
Or both have lost.

Love's Awakening

Awakened by the sun rays tapping on the window
Smiling by the sun rays tapping on the window
Smiling at fragrances of her body
The subtle sounds of her sleeping
Feeding my eyes with her beauty
Rubbing the back of my index finger across her face
Seeing her smile wrinkle activated
Warming my heart, lifting my spirits
Giving me the wings of freedom
Highlighting my destiny.

Love's Communication

Closing of your eyes when you kiss
Feeling that tingle of the confines to one another
Slowly the hands close around one another's
The solitude of the love call from a Native American flute
Drawing you into its consumption
Softly and subtle like an eagle in flight
Transcending the ages, floating there to touch the blueness
    of the sky
The flight into the unknown held together by love
Unrestrained smiles
Notness to unbelief
Togetherness a must through opposition
The starting of another day brings new hope.

Love Untouched

She doesn't know how much I love her
She doesn't know how much I care
The accidental touching, the accidental stares
When will she notice the trembling when I see her smile?
When she says hello, that it makes my day worthwhile
How long can it be a secret deep within my heart?
It shakes my very soul; it's tearing me apart.
When will I tell her, I've tried a thousand ways
Never-ending, everlasting, thoughts fill my days.

She satisfies my dreams of youth
Hinges those days of youthful truth
Laughter rings within my heart
I guess I've been smitten by Cupid's dart.

Not knowing what will lie ahead
I'm looking for unbroken love instead.

Mind's Eye View

I imagine, lost in her arms,
The feel and comfort of a warm fire
Is found there in that warm embrace
The flickering of light tries to bring forth
The mystery hidden in her disarming eyes
Her lips seem small as I view their curves around about
I love her tinkling bell voice, sweet and sincere
I listen intently at the happenings of her day
I give her an understanding smile
Watching the little wrinkle on her forehead
Disappear as she talks her tension away
Our hands touched, accidentally of course
I feel a tremor deep within my being
A smile appears, all is well of course.

Mindscapes

Tiptoeing through the destinies of fate
Watching them pile up in piles of nothingness
Their forgotten mindscapes
Feather dancing in slow motion as it falls to Earth
Bitfull information gathers dust while being a part of the
     whole
Locations of dry voices loathe one another.

Mirror Reflections

Ghosts of the future are mirrored from ghost of the past.
    Who are the players? Who are the cast?
A slight thing or large thing said, a gesture or an action.
    In a moment of anger or aggressive jesting and no
    retraction.
What a difference could have been done with "I'm sorry."
    Who said life's not a folly?

Who do you think we are playing with, a child's mind?
    Stuffing them full of garbage and keeping them in a
    bind.
Lose them to say, I love you and not to kill you in your
    sleep.
    Hatred can boil out of control and we die without a
    peep.

We die anyway when we say "I love you" and no answer
    is given.
    Holding out your arms for a hug and no response,
    you know you're not forgiven.
When I see your son and get a hug, to hold his little hand,
    I feel great pride as he says, "Grampa, I love you" and
    I feel grand.

Reaching into my bag of tricks, I win another basketball
    game.
    I fumble with the words "I guess I won," but Dad is
    not my name.
I reach into my mind for the right word for a smile,
    And maybe I can put together several words for a
    sentence to last awhile.

Maybe I can't help you forget the past,
But the future is in your son and it's fleeting so fast.
Maybe we can fog the mirror over to forever forget the ghosts,
To take away their haunts, to reach to the future and your son will be the host.

Moonbeam Treasures

Starry heavens
Held together by cosmic glue
Dawn's early light
Disappears into nothingness
Not to be retrieved until sunset's end
Ghostly figures appear until the moon's face glows
Unsure foot touches the sod below
Steps become familiar stepping on the moonbeam's ends
My friend the moon smiles down on me.

Moon Thoughts

Again I turn my face to the heavens
I see the moon's generous smile
The smile covers the distance between two lovers
Separated by fate
The distance is too far even to touch fingertips
They once held hands in his presence
I was there in his presence
Trying to read in the face what the future might hold
The clouds covered the moon's glow
I turned and went my way.

My Guitar

I played my guitar and heard nothing.
    Sang my song and broke a string.
With riddles and fittles I make my mark
    Two days on this song I'm ready to bark.

Playing intricate nothings I slipped and broke my nose
    Dropped my guitar and broke my toes
I can listen to Eric Clapton's blues
    Twisted and broken I'm paying my dues.

Mi Piture

The sound of the crayon skoots across my paper
Widening the perspective of my world
My mind's eye put on paper
My crooked lines are not what I see
Somehow gets the point across
Mommy with her sticklike legs
And shoes way too big
Flowers drawn on a red dress
A crooked toothless smile
The proudness of my efforts are hung for all to see
From the refrigerator low enough for me to see and touch.

My Secret Place

My secret place
Where the wind doesn't blow
No ice or snow.

A place of spring
Flowers in gentle array
Gentle breeze that causes a ripple on the lake.

A place where lovers can go
To meet their springtime needs
To touch those places in the heart
Feelings of love grow.

A place of no embarrassment
Words softly spoken
A soft touch
Laughter in the eyes.

I go here to pass my time
To write poems that tickle the heart
A place I hate to leave, for it's a part of me.

Not What I Was

Cross-eyed spectrum view interlacing joy and nausea
Emptying life-sustaining fluids into a generous commode
Loser's faith to try again
Undaunted life-support system hanging onto life's thread
Teetering of balance as you put one foot in front of the
    other
Unwanted need to reach for someone's support
Construction of thoughts builds to the point of recharging
Who is this person I've become?
Forever turned my back on this person
Now, not what I was.

Pillow Talk

I lay my head on my pillow at the end of the day
One more step into the future toward death's end.
Did I educate myself enough to offset life's tug-of-war
Youth and beauty, why can't they look like me?
Something I don't understand, I dissect, pick apart
Conclusions give comfort to my mind
To be shown in a different light to my best friend
Meanings change when maturity sets in.

Pleasantries

Candles, soft touch, soft kisses
Thoughts linger into pleasantries
Tummy tingles, a thousand butterflies flutter
What's the meaning of uncontrolled actions
Surrounded by thoughts too wonderful to speak?
Some say love.

Romeo's Beginning

Voice of voices, not Juliet's end
A newness of life
One that transcends a lover's life dreams
Met, matched, and built on
Governed not by self, but by emotions
Emotions that unlock the heart
Ones that enter the inner chambers
Where the tears of joy are stored
Opening floodgate of stored emotions of love
Guided by mind's eye viewing
The tingling feelings of touch
Knowing in your heart of hearts
The trust for one another
You say, "Romeo, Romeo, wherefore art thou?"
I, Romeo, will hold your hand,
Smoothing out the curves,
Walking through the valley of death's end.
And being elated by the conquering of the mountains.

Shhh, Listen

The lots were drawn
Falling on the most unlikely
Untalented but with determination
Scraps of paper covered the floor
Words came that didn't seem to match
Touching those subjects too sensitive to be spoken
Cast those lots to the sea
Chosen before time to write words of truth
Plucked from my mind's eye
Soft and warm to see and touch
Or creating fear of the unknown
Multi-grades of society break the stone tablets
They find comfort in the products of their environment
Taking toll of their lives.

Shoulder Vision

Things happen and I'm not at my best
Again I didn't pass the test
Life is moving smoothly until I look over my shoulder
I'm not at my best even if I'm a little bolder
Power plays and down plays are the spice of life
That's while I'm in the middle of my strife
Passive aggression confuses my mental resources
Dodging the verbal blows
Am I losing the race?
What are the goal's end rewards?
I draw up a win/loss column
Conclusion, I win.

Sleepless

Sleep is a premium to be coddled when it occurs
Counting sheep, dogs, cats, what's the difference?
They all end up doing funny things to make me laugh.
The more I try the wider my eyes become
Maybe if I exercise hopping on one foot, then the other
Reading can make one eye droop a little
The hours slip through endless nights
As I am forced to occupy my weary mind
With the thoughts of repose
And the days bring nothing but fatigue
Still, rest lies heavily on a broken dream
I am too tired to be awake
Yet I am too wakeful/restless to be asleep.

Smile

Unseen smile drifts away to nothingness
To have only seen that sun ray
Uplifting, subtle, showing storms gone by
How can you not draw attention to yourself
Revealing yourself with a smile?

Smiles

Enmesh particles of truth
Jeweler's duty
Lie that sparkles
That dims the truth
Smiles with discolored teeth
Arms tucked to sides
Covers stress
Shall we impeach?

Talents

My talents cry out to be heard
To make a difference to that someone
To turn a head while whispering thanks
To lighten a heavy heart
Plundering thoughts, pondering hearts
Opening eyes to a different light
A different world
Fantasies brought to life
Overlooked opportunities
Jelled magnitudes of pleasures released
If only to touch a soul, their needs released.

The Bully

Large in size and strength
Takes part of lunch and fun money
Doesn't like what you do or say
Wants you to change your way of thinking
Makes up his own rules
Nonconformist
I accepted his challenge on my own turf
He hadn't been beaten, I felt uneasy
We met face to face
I looked into his eyes of love
I had been beaten and fell to my knees
My broken spirit was lifted up
I became a part of him and he a part of me.

Toys of Thoughts

The toys of my thoughts play games with me
Tickling my heartbeat
Bringing thoughtful smiles
The light dancing in my eyes
Not looking for that heartache
But searching for lifelong experiences of joy
Eyes closed, thoughts drifting
Going into a limited equation of sleep
Joy is unlimited according to spent time.

Unjoy

Woman who with a smile draws me into her charms
What mysteries do you have hidden there
Keeping me unguarded from what life holds
Bolting the door behind me
For a while I feel secure
My quest drives me on
Your trials of another life
Tears are suppressed
Reaching your hand out to someone
That they might give you solace for what you hold within
Magnitudes of life's memories
Barren to joy
If only to live again.

Your Smile

The color of your smile lights the candle of my heart
Adjusting the glow spins tales of happiness
Passing the tones of forgotten grandeur of the past
Blanketed but not concealing the love that lingers from
    loves gone by
Lofting my thoughts only makes you more prominent
My strength leaves my knees
I grab your hand for support
And your smile lights that candle again.

Viewing from a Bottle

You view me as viewing from a bottle.
Floating on an ocean
Looking down on me being cast to and fro
Uninterrupted in my glass cage
There's nowhere to hide except within myself.

Vision

The stress of my everyday existence I've accepted as my
    dream
Constantly being aware of that individual who will push
    you over the top
Pyramiding through the rest of the day
Trying to pull those edges together
Fire dancing in my eyes, with my pasted-on smile
And a hint of growlance in my voice
My tunnel vision sees that special person standing at the
    end
Those quiet things that she does that are pleasant to me
She made my day.

What Am I?

Shyness to depression
Fate's hand
Glorified generosity
Conscious efforts
Gratitude to life's end
Enormous thought depths
Thought patterns emerge
Painted victory
Skinless personality
Now alone.

What Hurts?

Flaunting your criteria of useless words
Mumbling about your loves gone by
Trashing their intentions and motives
Letting them cut deep into the place where only you go
Lashing out to others as if they were the problem
Harboring deceit, after all they hurt you bad
What does a kind word mean to you?
Do you question what do they want?
Where will it end?
Then that babe walks by, you close your eyes
Maybe just one more try.

Words

Unsaid words roll from my mind's sanctuary
Piecing them into verbal sentences
Slowly at first, building into a cascade of excitement
Communication has started
Your interaction is all I need, what you think, feeling
Sharing that moment that only you know
Take from those fallacies I've formed
What about those diamond gems harbored in your heart?
Cross-linked those joys we have shared
Building on those mixed treasures.

Youthful Dreams

The dross of my life
Has poured down across my face
Leaving deep impressions there
Highly refined over the years
Impurities gone
Leaving a heart of gold
My hair the color of snow
As the snowflake, each one is an individual
Each one a reminder of a test I didn't pass
I see a beautiful woman walk by
Heart racing, I have a pill to slow it down
I smile as she walks on
Saying, "You dirty old man."
What happened to my youth
I still have inside me
Fighting the urges to become old
But I'm put into that box and put upon a shelf
Soon I'm forgotten
They say what happened to his youth?
I view the world around me
As only youthful dreams
And not touching on the reality of truth.

Youth in Nocturnalness

The uselessness of nursery rhymes
Driven as youth to find true meanings
The hangups of Humpty Dumpty
I walked to conformity's perimeters
Trying to peer over the constructed wall
What is beyond
It's higher than I can see
Who can hide an open mind?
Why is youth considered stupid?
It's only hidden by the breeding of concealing the truth.